You will always be loved my baby

SUSAN SCOTTFIELD

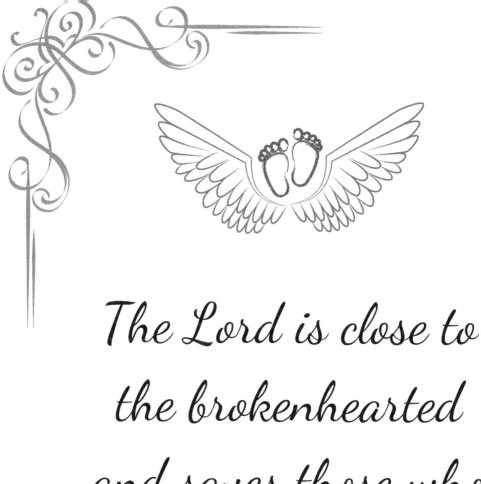

The Lord is close to the brokenhearted and saves those who are crushed in spirit

PSALM 34:18

Introduction

It is difficult to imagine a more traumatic event than the loss of a baby in pregnancy. This unexpected experience brings with it a sense of overwhelming pain and grief. It is a life-altering event that presents huge challenges to parents as they try to rebuild their lives without their precious baby.

It would be condescending to tell parents how to handle their loss, as we all express emotions in our own way. While this is the case, we must ask the question, how should Christians handle pregnancy loss? Does the Bible mention the subject and, if so, in what way?

There is some precedent in the Bible. Let's look at the example of David after losing his young son. Second Samuel 12:20 states:

> "Then David arose from the earth and washed and anointed himself and changed his clothes. And he went into the house of the Lord and worshiped. He then went to his own house. And when he asked, they set food before him, and he ate."

Here we see that David worshiped the Lord even after his son's death. Instead of abandoning his faith, David drew closer to God in his time of devastation.

In Second Samuel 12:23, David answers those who asked him about his response to his personal tragedy:

"But now he is dead. Why should I fast? Can I bring him back again? I shall go to him, but he will not return to me."

David realized that he could not do anything to alter the death of his child. However, he also knew that his child was now with God, in a place where David would eventually rejoin his son for eternity.

No parent will ever "get over" or "move on" from the loss of their baby. However, they can take comfort in scripture. One of the most revealing lessons is that children who die before they reach the age of accountability go to heaven.

David's response to those questioning his reaction has always been an immense source of comfort to Christian parents who have lost babies and young children. Recall the line "I will go to him, but he will not return to me" (2 Samuel 12:23). Here we see that David knew with complete certainty that he would meet his son in heaven. This passage is a powerful statement that babies and young children who pass over *will* go to heaven.

The Bible also makes clear that the overwhelming grief we are feeling now will not last forever. Though the sadness of a lost baby may be with you for life, there will come a day when the intense and crippling sorrow will end. Revelation 21:4 promises:

"He will wipe away every tear from their eyes, and death shall be no more, neither shall there be mourning, nor crying, nor pain anymore, for the former things have passed away."

Grieving the death of a baby is a difficult journey. There are no hard and fast rules on how to handle our mourning. However, pastors, counselors and those who have lost a baby point to the need to have an outlet to express feelings. Here's where this journal comes in.

How to use this book

This journal contains 50 Bible quotes that have been specially selected for their power and relevance to loss and grief. Alongside each quote is a blank page entitled 'Words from my heart'.

I would ask you to read the Bible quote and then write your thoughts and feelings on the page opposite. This journaling can be based on the quote you have read or could be any thoughts and feelings that come to you in the moment.

Free your mind and free your hand to connect with your heart and put onto paper what you need to let out.

Please be honest and raw – this is not the time to be polite. As Christians, we (quite rightly) value civility, moderation and temperance, which are all noble qualities. However, this is your personal and private journal — **for your eyes only**. To experience the best healing effect, you need to let your feelings out. Even if they are dark. Even if you question your faith. Even if you feel you have been forsaken by God. Express it. Let it out.

Keep in mind Proverbs 3:5-6:

*Trust in the Lord with all your heart
and lean not on your own understanding;
in all your ways submit to him,
and he will make your paths straight.*

Some days you might want to right a simple, short statement. Other times you will want to write your heart out. Follow your instincts. Write what comes naturally to you.

After you have read all 50 verses and filled all 50 pages with your thoughts, I am confident that, with God's grace, you will be in a better place. Keep this journal close to you.

I sincerely hope the Bible verses bring you peace, comfort and solace in your time of need, while your journaling allows you release, respite and a lightening of your burden.

Wishing you love and light.

Susan Scottfield

For You created my inmost being; You knit me in my mother's womb. I praise You because I am fearfully and wonderfully made

Psalm 139: 13-14

Words from my heart

Brothers and sisters, we do not want you to be uninformed about those who sleep in death, so that you do not grieve like the rest of mankind, who have no hope. For since we believe that Jesus died and rose again, we also believe that God will bring with Jesus those who have fallen asleep in Him

Thessalonians 4:13

Words from my heart

He will wipe every tear from their eyes. There will be no more death or mourning or crying or pain, for the old order of things has passed away

REVELATION 21:4

Words from my heart

The Lord is close to the brokenhearted and saves those who are crushed in spirit

Psalm 34:18

Words from my heart

Blessed are those who mourn, for they shall be comforted

MATTHEW 5:4

Words from my heart

Do not sorrow, for the joy of the Lord is your strength

NEHEMIAH 8:10

Words from my heart

Therefore we do not lose heart. For our light and momentary troubles are achieving for us an eternal glory that far outweighs them all. So we fix our eyes not on what is seen, but on what is unseen, since what is seen is temporary, but what is unseen is eternal

2 Corinthians 4:16-18

Words from my heart

He heals the brokenhearted and binds up their wounds

PSALM 147:3

Words from my heart

My flesh and my heart may fail, but God is the strength of my heart and my portion forever

Psalm 73:26

Words from my heart

And we know that in all things God works for the good of those who love Him, who have been called according to His purpose

Romans 8:28

Words from my heart

The last enemy to be destroyed is death

1 CORINTHIANS 15:26

Words from my heart

Give all your worries to Him, because He cares for you

1 PETER 5:7

Words from my heart

But the Lord is faithful, and He will strengthen and protect you from the evil one

2 THESSALONIANS 3:3

Words from my heart

The Lord your God will go with you. He will not leave you or forget you

DEUTERONOMY 31:6

Words from my heart

The Lord is the one who goes ahead of you; He will be with you. He will not fail you or forsake you. Do not fear or be dismayed

DEUTERONOMY 31:8

Words from my heart

We can say with confidence, "The Lord is my helper; I will not be afraid. What can anyone do to me?"

HEBREWS 13:6

Words from my heart

He gives strength to the weary and increases the power of the weak

ISAIAH 40:29

Words from my heart

Do not fear, for I am with you; Do not anxiously look about you, for I am your God. I will strengthen you, surely I will help you, Surely I will uphold you with My righteous right hand

ISAIAH 41:10

Words from my heart

For the mountains may depart and the hills be removed, but my steadfast love shall not depart from you

ISAIAH 54:10

Words from my heart

The Spirit of the Sovereign Lord is on me, because the Lord has anointed me to proclaim good news to the poor. He has sent me to bind up the brokenhearted, to proclaim freedom for the captives and release from darkness for the prisoners

Isaiah 61:1

Words from my heart

I have loved you with an everlasting love; I have drawn you with unfailing kindness

JEREMIAH 31:3

Words from my heart

You will feel safe because there is hope

JOB 11:18

Words from my heart

For God so loved the world that He gave His only begotten Son, that whoever believes in Him should not perish but have everlasting life

JOHN 3:16

Words from my heart

You came near when I called on you; you said, "Do not fear!"

LAMENTATIONS 3:57

Words from my heart

You have taken up my cause, O Lord; you have redeemed my life

LAMENTATIONS 3:58

Words from my heart

He has sent Me [Jesus] to heal the brokenhearted

LUKE 4:18

Words from my heart

Blessed are you who weep now, for you will laugh

LUKE 6:21

Words from my heart

I love the Lord, because He hears My voice and my supplications

PSALM 116:1

Words from my heart

Your word is a lamp to my feet, and a light to my path

PSALM 119:105

Words from my heart

You are my hiding place and my shield. I hope in your word

PSALM 119:114

Words from my heart

This is my comfort in my affliction, That Your word has revived me.

PSALM 119:50

Words from my heart

Let your steadfast love comfort me according to your promise to your servant

PSALM 119:76

Words from my heart

The Lord shall preserve you from all evil; He shall preserve your soul

PSALM 121:7

Words from my heart

The Lord is gracious and full of compassion

PSALM 145:8

Words from my heart

The Lord is my rock, my fortress and my deliverer; my God is my rock, in whom I take refuge, my shield and the horn of my salvation, my stronghold

Psalm 18:2

Words from my heart

My God turns my darkness into light

PSALM 18:28

Words from my heart

Even though I walk through the darkest valley, I will fear no evil, for you are with me; your rod and your staff, they comfort me

PSALM 23:4

Words from my heart

The Lord is my light and my salvation; whom shall I fear? The Lord is the stronghold of my life; of whom shall I be afraid?

PSALM 27:1

Words from my heart

I remain confident of this: I will see the goodness of the Lord in the land of the living

PSALM 27:13

But the salvation of the righteous is from the Lord; He is their strength in the time of trouble

PSALM 37:39

Words from my heart

God is our protection and our strength. He always helps in times of trouble

Psalm 46:1

Words from my heart

You have recorded my troubles. You have kept a list of my tears. Aren't they in your records?

PSALM 56:8

Words from my heart

On the day I call for help, my enemies will be defeated. I know that God is on my side

Psalm 56:9

Words from my heart

You are my protection, my place of safety in times of trouble

PSALM 59:16

Words from my heart

From the ends of the earth I call to you, I call as my heart grows faint; lead me to the rock that is higher than I

Psalm 61:2

Words from my heart

My soul, wait in silence for God only, For my hope is from Him.

PSALM 62:5

Words from my heart

Yet I am always with you; you hold me by my right hand

PSALM 73:23

Words from my heart

Give me a sign of your goodness, that my enemies may see it and be put to shame, for you, Lord, have helped me and comforted me

PSALM 86:17

Words from my heart

Now may the God of hope fill you with all joy and peace in believing, so that you will abound in hope by the power of the Holy Spirit

ROMANS 15:13

Words from my heart

The Lord your God in your midst, The Mighty One, will save; He will rejoice over you with gladness, He will quiet you with His love, He will rejoice over you with singing

ZEPHANIAH 3:17

Words from my heart

Made in the USA
Monee, IL
24 November 2020